Wake Up And Praise!

An Invitation to Experience God's Glory

Barbara Lyons Slade

ISBN:	Softcover	978-1-6698-3735-0
	eBook	978-1-6698-3734-3

Print information available on the last page.

Rev. date: 07/25/2022

To order additional copies of this book, contact:
Xlibris
844-714-8691
www.Xlibris.com
Orders@Xlibris.com
841224

Contents

Acknowledgements

*My deepest gratitude to my dear friend
and editor, Trudy Graves. Thank you for your
unwavering dedication and hard work to help me
accomplish what the Lord has called me to do.
I pray God's richest blessings upon your life.*

*And to my Heavenly Father, to whom I give
all honor and glory, adoration and praise.*

*"Blessed is Your name forever and forever;
from sunrise to sunset!
For You are high above the nations;
Your glory is far greater than the heavens."
Psalm 113:2-4 TLB*

The people whom I formed for
Myself will make known My praise.
Isaiah 43:21 AMP

Praise lifts us beyond our experiences and connects us to the One who has displayed Himself through our experiences. We get to honor God in light of what He has done.

In "Wake Up and Praise!" we rehearse and internalize the wondrous works of God, feeding our souls a constant, refreshening stream of His life. As His life cascades throughout our being, we have an assurance of spiritual vibrancy and a fruit-bearing life.

Dorothy Marie Scott,
Pastor and Founder of Kingdom Life Movement, Inc.

How to Use
"WAKE UP AND PRAISE!"

Each section includes four pages that begin with scripture and end with prayer.

1. Begin by thanking God for Jesus, His loving-kindness, and grace. Thank Him for the ability to read and understand the things of God and for the privilege to praise Him freely.

2. Read the **Scriptures** that are before the Prophetic Affirmations page. Read each word slowly. Ask the Holy Spirit to speak to you. Take time to listen and write down whatever He says.

3. Speak the **Prophetic Affirmations** <u>ALOUD</u>. As you speak them repeatedly and with intent, they will renew your mind, increase your faith, and strengthen you to do the things God created you to do. Be sure to read the motivational prompts in between each set of affirmations.

4. Read the **Words of Inspiration** for encouragement and insight.

5. Lift your voice in **Prayerful Praise**. These prayers focus more on the goodness and greatness of God rather than petitions and intercessions. They are formatted to keep your spirit engaged in praise and thanksgiving.

Whoever offers praise glorifies Me.
Psalm 50:23 NKJV

So we, Your people and sheep
of Your pasture, will give You
thanks forever; We will show forth
Your praise to all generations.
Psalm 79:13 NKJV

Wake Up And Praise!

An Invitation to Experience God's Glory

The God Most High accomplishes
all things on my behalf [for He
completes my purpose in His plan].
Psalm 57:2 AMP

Great is the Lord! He is most
worthy of praise! No one can
measure his greatness.
Psalm 145:3 NLT

1

A Life Worth Living

Prophetic Affirmations

I thank God for accomplishing all things on my behalf.
I thank God for completing my purpose in His plan.
I thank God for another chance to do His will.
I thank God for giving me a life worth living.

Declare these words with gratitude and intent.
Inspire yourself by what you hear.

I thank God for accomplishing all things on my behalf.
I thank God for completing my purpose in His plan.
I thank God for another chance to do His will.
I thank God for giving me a life worth living.

Speak the words once more. Use your voice
to equip yourself. There is power and
purpose in what you say!

I thank God for accomplishing all things on my behalf.
I thank God for completing my purpose in His plan.
I thank God for another chance to do His will.
I thank God for giving me a life worth living.

Embrace each day as a gift, a chance to realize a dream, achieve a goal or do something fun, memorable, extraordinary, or meaningful. Welcome each day as an opportunity to make a difference in someone else's life, which is God's will for those in Christ. According to Ephesians 2:10 TLB, "It is God himself who has made us what we are and given us new lives from Christ Jesus and that we should spend these lives helping others."

Some people need what you have, just as there are people who have what you need. It could be praying for someone, sharing words of comfort, providing transportation, warm clothes, a meal, or just conversation. It can also be sharing your gifts and talents with others. The list is endless.

Depend on God to show you what to do and where to go. Listen for His voice through prayer, insight, and revelation. God will lead you in the right direction and give you divine connections. Consider nothing as coincidence but as the providence of God, then step out in faith as you hear from Him. Praise God for the plans He has for your life. Thank God for giving you a life worth living!

Prayerful Praise

Holy Father,
Creator of the world,
Thank You for the gift of life.
Thank You for the day I was born and
for the plans You ordained for me.

Holy Father,
Thank You for showing me the way
I should go and the paths I should take.
Thank You for orchestrating my days
and securing my divine destiny.

Holy Father,
Thank You for helping me live
a productive and purposeful life.
Thank You for giving me a life worth living.
You are an awesome God
and most worthy of praise.
Hallelujah and Amen!

O Sovereign Lord! You made the heavens and earth by your strong hand and powerful arm. Nothing is too hard for you!
Jeremiah 32:17 NLT

I know that you can do anything, and no one can stop you.
Job 42:2 NLT

2

All Things Are Possible

Prophetic Affirmations

I praise God for His sovereignty.
I praise God for His infinite greatness.
I praise God for His mighty power.
I praise God because He can do anything.

*Say these words again. God is pleased
with our expressions of praise.*

I praise God for His sovereignty.
I praise God for His infinite greatness.
I praise God for His mighty power.
I praise God because He can do anything.

*Keep talking. Encourage yourself
by what you say. Increase your
faith by what you hear.*

I praise God for His sovereignty.
I praise God for His infinite greatness.
I praise God for His mighty power.
I praise God because He can do anything.

God transcends powers and principalities.
He is sovereign over all that exists.
He is unparalleled in strength and majestic in victory.
All things are possible with Him.

God is holy, invincible, and infinite.
He created the entire world at His command.
He is almighty, immovable, and unchanging.
All things are possible with Him.

The Lord is omnipotent, self-existent, and all-wise.
He holds time and eternity in His hands.
He is glorious, excellent, marvelous, and awesome.
All things are possible with Him.

God reigns over the heavens and all its hosts.
He is above all, before all, and no one counsels Him.
He is the Alpha and Omega, the First and the Last.
All things are possible with Him.

Prayerful Praise

Sovereign Lord,
Ruler of the universe,
All things are possible with You.

Sovereign Lord,
No one can stop what You have started.
No one can undo what You have planned.
You will complete what You have established.
Everything You say will come to pass.

Sovereign Lord,
Your ways are glorious.
Your works are perfect.
All things are possible with You.
Hallelujah and Amen!

*Don't copy the behavior and
customs of this world, but let God
transform you into a new person
by changing the way you think.*
Romans 12:2 NLT

*And whatever you do, whether in
word or deed, do it all in the name of
the Lord Jesus, giving thanks to
God the Father through him.*
Colossians 3:17 NIV

3

An Attitude of Gratitude

Prophetic Affirmations

I thank God for teaching me to renew my mind.
I thank God for helping me to have a right attitude.
I thank God for helping me to keep my mind on Jesus.
I thank God for helping me to do things His way.

Speak these words again slowly.
Strengthen your mind by what you say.

I thank God for teaching me to renew my mind.
I thank God for helping me to have a right attitude.
I thank God for helping me to keep my mind on Jesus.
I thank God for helping me to do things His way.

Repeat these words over and over.
Speak aloud so you can hear what you say.
Be transformed by the words of your mouth.

I thank God for teaching me to renew my mind.
I thank God for helping me to have a right attitude.
I thank God for helping me to keep my mind on Jesus.
I thank God for helping me to do things His way.

Begin your day with the right attitude by
renewing your mind with thoughts of gratitude.
Take a moment to remember what God has done.
He secured our future through the life of His Son.

Fix your mind on Jesus and what He did at Calvary.
Let the glory of His sacrifice put your mind at ease.
Quiet your thoughts and meditate on God's grace.
Whatever happens in life, with God, you can face.

Spend time with God, read the Bible and pray,
then wait to hear what the Holy Spirit will say.
Praise God for giving you another day.
Praise God for helping you to do things His way.

Prayerful Praise

Heavenly Father,
God of Glory and Grace,
Forgive me for the times I started my
day with a wrong attitude, when
my heart was in the wrong place, or
when I thought more about what I
wanted than what was best for me.

Heavenly Father,
Thank You for helping me to
keep my mind on Jesus.
Thank You for teaching me to
listen to the Holy Spirit.
Thank You for helping me to do things
Your way and to honor You with my life.
In Jesus' name

*In every situation [no matter what
the circumstances] be thankful and
continually give thanks to God; for this
is the will of God for you in Christ Jesus.
1 Thessalonians 5:18 AMP*

*Oh, how grateful and thankful
I am to the Lord because he is so good.
I will sing praise to the name of the
Lord who is above all lords.
Psalm 7:17 TLB*

4

Be Thankful

Prophetic Affirmations

I thank God in every situation.
I continually give thanks to the Lord.
I am grateful for all that God does for me.
I am thankful because God is so good.

Speak the words over and over until you
feel the weight of the words in your soul.
Be inspired by what you say.

I thank God in every situation.
I continually give thanks to the Lord.
I am grateful for all that God does for me.
I am thankful because God is so good.

Speak the words again.
Be blessed by what you hear.

I thank God in every situation.
I continually give thanks to the Lord.
I am grateful for all that God does for me.
I am thankful because God is so good.

Thank God in every situation.
Thank God in the ups and downs of life.
Thank God in the humdrum of daily duties.
Thank God when life is big, bold, and bright.

Thank God for the unfolding of opportunities.
Thank God for the blessings He gives you each day.
Thank God for what He created you to do.
Thank God for the life He has planned for you.

Thank God because the scriptures tell us to do so.
Thank God because it is righteousness unto Him.
Thank God because it is you He intends to bless.
Thank God because He is worthy of nothing less.

Prayerful Praise

Lord God Almighty,
Faithful and True God,
Sovereign Lord and Savior,
Holy is Your name.

Lord God Almighty,
There are not enough words to express
my gratitude for all that You do for me.
In the morning, You greet me with new mercies.
In the evening, You are still with me,
blessing me in more ways than I can count.

Lord God Almighty,
Thank You for blessing me at all
times and in every way.
You are an awesome God, a mighty
Father, and a perfect Savior.
I bless Your holy name.
Hallelujah and Amen!

*You have turned my mourning
into dancing for me; you have
taken off my sackcloth and
clothed me with joy, that my
soul may sing praise to you and
not be silent. O Lord my God,
I will give thanks to you forever.
Psalm 30:10-12 AMP*

*He helps me, and my
heart is filled with joy.
Psalm 28:7 NLT*

5

Clothed With Joy

Prophetic Affirmations

I bless God for strengthening my heart.
I bless God for clothing me with joy.
I bless God for turning my mourning into dancing.
I bless God for giving me a song of praise.

Consistently reminding yourself of the
goodness of God will help you recognize
the goodness of God. Keep speaking.

I bless God for strengthening my heart.
I bless God for clothing me with joy.
I bless God for turning my mourning into dancing.
I bless God for giving me a song of praise.

Speak the words again aloud.
Create an atmosphere of praise by what you say.

I bless God for strengthening my heart.
I bless God for clothing me with joy.
I bless God for turning my mourning into dancing.
I bless God for giving me a song of praise.

God turns our mourning into dancing.
He gives us songs for our sorrow.
He helps us praise Him through our pain.
God gives us hope for a better tomorrow.

God turns our troubles into testimonies.
He gives us strength when times are hard.
He helps us praise Him in our suffering.
God calms the anxieties in our hearts.

God turns our sadness into joy.
He gives us grace when we are grieving.
He helps us praise Him when life seems cold.
God soothes the agony in our souls.

God turns our problems into purpose.
He gives us peace for all concerns.
He helps us praise Him in our difficulties.
God shows us favor at every turn.

Prayerful Praise

Most High God,
Lord of lords and King of kings,
Sovereign God above all things,
I bless Your holy name.

Most High God,
Thank You for giving me hope when
life seems dark and unbearable.
Thank You for blessing me with courage
when I feel I have no strength.
Thank You for clothing me with joy when
my soul is overcome with sorrow.

Most High God,
Lord of lords and King of kings,
Sovereign God above all things,
I thank You, I praise You, and I bless You.
In Jesus' holy name

Then God said, "Let us make a man—
someone like ourselves, to be the
master of all life upon the earth and
in the skies and in the seas."
Genesis 1:26 TLB

Then the Lord God formed a man from
the dust of the ground and breathed
into his nostrils the breath of life,
and the man became a living being.
Genesis 2:7 NIV

6

Created in His Image

Prophetic Affirmations

I praise God for making me in His image.
I praise God for giving me life.
I praise God for creating me for greatness.
I praise God for helping me to live my life for Him.

Empower yourself by what you say.
God has great plans for you.

I praise God for making me in His image.
I praise God for giving me life.
I praise God for creating me for greatness.
I praise God for helping me to live my life for Him.

Keep speaking.
Align your words with the scriptures.
Speak words that agree with God.

I praise God for making me in His image.
I praise God for giving me life.
I praise God for creating me for greatness.
I praise God for helping me to live my life for Him.

God created us in His image.
He made us a little lower than the angels.
He gave us dominion over the works of His hands.
He designed us to fellowship with Him.

God made us to rule the earth.
He crowned us with glory and honor.
He gave us the right to become His children.
He planned for us to live eternally with Him.

God formed us to do good works.
He set us apart for His purposes.
He gave us His Spirit to help us live righteously.
God created us to praise and worship Him.

Prayerful Praise

Heavenly Father,
Creator of the world,
Sustainer of all living things,
I bless Your marvelous name.
Please help me to appreciate
each day and to enjoy the beauty of the
sunrise, the glow of the night sky, the breeze
in the trees, and all that You have created.
But most importantly, help me to
appreciate the miracle of me.

Heavenly Father,
Thank You for creating me in Your image
and for giving me a life worth living.
My soul rejoices in Your plans for me
and to You alone, I offer my praise.
In Jesus' mighty name

Do not fear [anything], for I am
with you; Do not be afraid, for I am
your God; I will strengthen you,
be assured I will help you.
Isaiah 41:10 AMP

The Lord is my strength and my shield;
My heart trusted in Him, and I am helped;
Therefore my heart greatly rejoices,
And with my song I will praise Him.
Psalm 28:7 NKJV

7

Destined to Win

Prophetic Affirmations

I bless God because He is always with me.
I bless God because He is always on my side.
I bless God because He is always ready to help me.
I bless God because He makes me strong in Him.

*Repeat the statements. The more you
infuse yourself with words of praise and
thanksgiving, the stronger you will become.*

I bless God because He is always with me.
I bless God because He is always on my side.
I bless God because He is always ready to help me.
I bless God because He makes me strong in Him.

*Keep speaking until you believe
that you are destined to win.*

I bless God because He is always with me.
I bless God because He is always on my side.
I bless God because He is always ready to help me.
I bless God because He makes me strong in Him.

The Bible does not say that life will be easy. On the contrary, John 16:33 TLB tells us, "Here on earth we will have many trials and sorrows. But cheer up, for I [Jesus] have overcome the world."

Since Jesus Himself gave this word of knowledge and comfort, let us not be taken aback when hard times come. Troubles can strengthen us, increase our faith, and deepen our relationship with God.

Our heavenly Father is a present help in trouble, and He will never leave us nor forsake us. He will be with us during times of sorrow, hardships, and tragedies. The Lord will equip and empower us to rise above every struggle. He will fight our battles and cause us to triumph in Him.

Praise God because our Creator never planned for us to live apart from Him or struggle in this life without His help. He is always on our side and works all things for our good. Praise Him because we are more than conquerors in Christ. Praise Him because no matter what life brings, Jesus has paid the price and has overcome the world.

Prayerful Praise

Heavenly Father,
Faithful and True God,
Mighty and majestic in power,
Everything You do is worthy of praise.

Your perfect plan of salvation and
redemption is worthy of praise.
Your excellent plan of victory
through Jesus is worthy of praise.
Everything You do is worthy of praise.

Your promise to fight my battles
is worthy of praise.
Your promise to always be on my
side is worthy of praise.
Your promise to work all things out
for my good is worthy of praise.

Heavenly Father,
Everything You do is worthy of praise.
Hallelujah and Amen!

*In My Father's house are many
mansions; if it were not so, I would
have told you. I go to prepare a
place for you. And if I go and prepare
a place for you, I will come again
and receive you to Myself; that
where I am, there you may be also.
John 14:2-3 NKJV*

*Whoever hears my word and believes
him who sent me has eternal life.
John 5:24 NIV*

8

Eternal Life With God

Prophetic Affirmations

I praise God for a glorious future.
I praise God for eternal life with Him.
I praise God for my divine destiny.
I praise God for preparing a place for me.

*Speaking these words aloud will
help diminish negative thoughts
that come from the cares of this world.*

I praise God for a glorious future.
I praise God for eternal life with Him.
I praise God for my divine destiny.
I praise God for preparing a place for me.

*Speak the words again.
Encourage yourself by what you say.*

I praise God for a glorious future.
I praise God for eternal life with Him.
I praise God for my divine destiny.
I praise God for preparing a place for me.

Your eternal life with God is a place where
there are no shattered dreams or broken promises.
You will not experience sadness or grief.
Troubles and afflictions no longer exist,
and loneliness is a thing of the past.

Your eternal life with God is a place without
sickness, despair, or discouragement.
You will never struggle with fear or anxiety.
Pain and sorrow have ceased to be;
and death and destruction are gone forever.

Your eternal life with God is a place
Jesus has gone to prepare for you!

For no eye has seen, no ear has heard,
and no mind has imagined what God has
prepared for those who love him.
1 Corinthians 2:9 NLT

Prayerful Praise

Holy and Awesome God,
All-Powerful and Faithful Father,
I am so glad that this life is only temporary
and that You have planned a glorious
future for those who live in Christ.
I would be without hope if this were not true.

Holy and Awesome God,
All-Powerful and Faithful Father,
I believe Your Word and the
wonderful life You have ordained for me.
Thank You for the promise of eternal life.
Thank You for eternal joy.
Thank You for eternal peace.
Thank You for eternal life with You.
Hallelujah and Amen!

The Almighty is beyond our
reach and exalted in power.
Job 37:23 NIV

His glory is far more vast than the
heavens. It towers above the earth.
Psalm 108:5 TLB

Be still, and know that I am God;
I will be exalted among the nations,
I will be exalted in the earth.
Psalm 46:10 NIV

9

Exalt God Above All

Prophetic Affirmations

I exalt God above people and places.
I exalt God above principalities and powers.
I exalt God above kingdoms and nations.
I exalt God above all things.

*Speaking words about God will
increase your desire for God.*

I exalt God above people and places.
I exalt God above principalities and powers.
I exalt God above kingdoms and nations.
I exalt God above all things.

*Repeat the words aloud.
Use your voice to draw closer to God.
Use your voice to praise the Lord.*

I exalt God above people and places.
I exalt God above principalities and powers.
I exalt God above kingdoms and nations.
I exalt God above all things.

World leaders have a platform that can promote peace or cause unrest in our lives. Others in government, city and judicial positions can alter our lives without notice. And those dominant in our workplaces, homes, and schools can either enrich us or bring harm to our well-being.

The Bible also tells us in Ephesians 6:12 (paraphrased) "that our struggle is not only against mankind, but against rulers, authorities, and spiritual forces of evil in the heavenly realms."

The good news is that no matter who they are or what position they hold, God is higher, His name is greater, and His works are more powerful. He transcends people, places, nations, and kingdoms now and forever. He is the Alpha and Omega, First and the Last, the Beginning and the End, which makes Him worthy of exaltation. He is the Lord God Almighty, and He is the One we praise!

Prayerful Praise

Holy God,
Lord of lords and King of kings,
Omnipotent Father and God Omniscient,
Great and mighty are You, Lord.

Holy God,
Everything that has breath is subject to You.
Every situation is under Your authority.
There is no one more powerful than You.
Great and mighty are You, Lord.

Holy God,
You are higher than the highest heavens.
Your power reigns throughout the universe.
There is no one above You or before You.
Great and mighty are You, Lord.

Hallelujah, Hallelujah!
Great and mighty are You, Lord.

*Yours, Lord, is the greatness
and the power and the glory and
the majesty and the splendor,
for everything in heaven
and earth is yours.
1 Chronicles 29:11 NIV*

*Be exalted, O God, above the
highest heavens! May your glory
shine over all the earth.
Psalm 57:5 NLT*

10

Glory to God

Prophetic Affirmations

I exalt God because He is sovereign.
I exalt God because He is great.
I exalt God because He is all-powerful.
I exalt God because He is good.

There is power in what you say.
There is power when you speak words
that exalt the Lord.

I exalt God because He is sovereign.
I exalt God because He is great.
I exalt God because He is all-powerful.
I exalt God because He is good.

Keep speaking.
Bless yourself by the words of your mouth.

I exalt God because He is sovereign.
I exalt God because He is great.
I exalt God because He is all-powerful.
I exalt God because He is good.

When you speak words about God's greatness,
it brings glory to God, for He, Himself has said,

"I am the Lord; that is my name!
I will not yield my glory to another."
Isaiah 42:8 NIV

When you speak words about God's power,
it brings glory to God, for He, Himself has said,

"I am the first and I am the last;
apart from me there is no God."
Isaiah 44:6 NIV

When you speak words about God's sovereignty,
it brings glory to God, for He, Himself has said,

"I am the Lord, and there is no other."
Isaiah 45:6 NIV

Prayerful Praise

Most High God,
Sovereign King and Lord,
All glory belongs to You.
Bless Your holy name.

Most High God,
All power belongs to You.
You alone made the world and all that is in it.
Everything in heaven and earth is Yours.
Bless Your holy name.

Most High God,
There is no one greater than You.
There is no one more worthy of praise.
Bless Your holy name.
Hallelujah and Amen!

The Lord always keeps his promises;
he is gracious in all he does.
Psalm 145:13 NLT

I praise God for what he has promised.
Psalm 56:10 NLT

I will praise you, Lord, with all
my heart; I will tell of all the
marvelous things you have done.
Psalm 9:1 NLT

11

God Keeps His Promises

Prophetic Affirmations

I bless the Lord because He is a promise keeper.
I bless the Lord because He is a miracle worker.
I bless the Lord because He is a bondage breaker.
I bless the Lord because He is a way maker.

The more you speak these words over your life,
the more belief you will instill in yourself.

I bless the Lord because He is a promise keeper.
I bless the Lord because He is a miracle worker.
I bless the Lord because He is a bondage breaker.
I bless the Lord because He is a way maker.

Repeat the words once more.
Be empowered by what you say.
Repetition is the key.

I bless the Lord because He is a promise keeper.
I bless the Lord because He is a miracle worker.
I bless the Lord because He is a bondage breaker.
I bless the Lord because He is a way maker.

God is a promise keeper.
He will watch over His Word to fulfill it.
He will bring to pass whatever He has spoken.
He cannot deny Himself, and He cannot lie.
Everything God says is true.

God is a way maker.
He will provide for us in unexpected ways,
open doors where we only see obstacles,
and work all things out for our good.
God can do anything.

God is a miracle worker.
He can reverse conditions, heal our bodies, raise
the dead, and deliver us from spiritual darkness.
Nothing is too hard for the One we worship!
Nothing is impossible for the God we praise!

Prayerful Praise

Heavenly Father,
Holy and Faithful God,
Thank You for doing the miraculous,
the impossible, and the extraordinary.

Thank You for making a way
when I could not see a solution.
Thank You for showing me Your favor and
providing for me in unexpected ways.
Thank You, most of all, for Your Word
and Your faithfulness towards me.

Heavenly Father,
I praise You because You do what You say.
I praise You because You do all things well.
I praise You because You are God.
Hallelujah and Amen!

Lord, you are my God;
I will exalt you and praise your name,
for in perfect faithfulness, you have done
wonderful things, things planned long ago.
Isaiah 25:1 NIV

I will praise the Lord, and may
everyone on earth bless his holy
name forever and ever.
Psalm 145:21 NLT

12

God Will Bless You

Prophetic Affirmations

I exalt the Lord's name because He is mighty.
I exalt the Lord's name because He is good.
I exalt the Lord's name because He is faithful.
I exalt the Lord's name because He is God.

Keep talking about exalting God's name.
Keep speaking words that will fortify your soul.

I exalt the Lord's name because He is mighty.
I exalt the Lord's name because He is good.
I exalt the Lord's name because He is faithful.
I exalt the Lord's name because He is God.

Speak the words again slowly.
Use your voice to bless yourself.
There is power in what you say.

I exalt the Lord's name because He is mighty.
I exalt the Lord's name because He is good.
I exalt the Lord's name because He is faithful.
I exalt the Lord's name because He is God.

God delights in your words of adoration.
God welcomes your expressions of thanks.
The Lord loves to hear your songs of praise.
God blesses you because you acknowledge His name.

God takes pleasure in your fellowship.
God is happy when you spend time with Him.
God bends His ear to hear your words of praise.
God blesses you because you honor His name.

God treasures your spirit of worship.
The Lord rejoices when you make room for Him.
God is pleased with the sacrifice of your praise.
God will bless you because you exalt His name.

Prayer of Praise

Great and Mighty God,
Everlasting Father,
You are above all and before all.
There is none like You.

Great and Mighty God,
Eternal Lord,
You are Ruler of the universe.
There is none like You.

Great and Mighty God,
Sovereign Lord and Savior,
You transcend every living thing.
There is none like You.

Great and Mighty God,
You are worthy of the highest praise.
In Jesus' holy and mighty name,
Hallelujah and Amen!

*Before anything else existed,
there was Christ, with God. He has
always been alive and is himself God.
He created everything there is—
nothing exists that he didn't make.
John 1:1-3 TLB*

*For God's secret plan, now at last
made known, is Christ himself.
Colossians 2:2 TLB*

13

God's Beloved Son

Prophetic Affirmations

I exalt Jesus because He is supreme over all creation.
I exalt Jesus because He existed before anything else.
I exalt Jesus because He is the visible image of God.
I exalt Jesus because He is God's beloved Son.

Jesus is so much more than we perceive.
Keep talking about His supremacy
and let the truth encourage you.

I exalt Jesus because He is supreme over all creation.
I exalt Jesus because He existed before anything else.
I exalt Jesus because He is the visible image of God.
I exalt Jesus because He is God's beloved Son.

Speak the words again aloud and with
confidence. Jesus is honored by what you say!

I exalt Jesus because He is supreme over all creation.
I exalt Jesus because He existed before anything else.
I exalt Jesus because He is the visible image of God.
I exalt Jesus because He is God's beloved Son.

"Christ is the visible image of the invisible God. He existed before anything was created and is supreme over all creation, for through him God created everything in the heavenly realms and on earth. He made the things we can see and the things we can't see, such as thrones, kingdoms, rulers, and authorities in the unseen world. Everything was created through him and for him. He existed before anything else, and he holds all creation together."

"Christ is also the head of the church, which is his body. He is the beginning, supreme over all who rise from the dead. So he is first in everything. For God in all his fullness was pleased to live in Christ, and through him God reconciled everything to himself. He made peace with everything in heaven and on earth by means of Christ's blood on the cross." (Colossians 1:15-20 NLT)

Prayerful Praise

Heavenly Father,
God of heaven and earth,
Father of the Lord Jesus Christ,
I praise Your holy name.

Heavenly Father,
Thank You for Your gracious
and merciful plan of reconciliation.
Thank You for Jesus who is
the visible image of You.

Heavenly Father,
With my whole heart, I exalt You
and thank You for Your mighty works.
In the name of Jesus,
I bless You and I praise You.
Hallelujah and Amen!

This is love: not that we loved God,
but that he loved us and sent his Son
as an atoning sacrifice for our sins.
1 John 4:10-11 NIV

For God so loved the world that
He gave His only begotten Son, that
whoever believes in Him should not
perish but have everlasting life.
John 3:16 NKJV

14

Greatest Love of All

Prophetic Affirmations

I thank God for His great love.
I thank God for His sacrificial love.
I thank God for His unconditional love.
I thank God for His perfect love.

Talking about God's love will help
you to embrace the greatness of God's love.

I thank God for His great love.
I thank God for His sacrificial love.
I thank God for His unconditional love.
I thank God for His perfect love.

Say the words "I thank God" over
and over, then speak the affirmations
again and be blessed by what you say.

I thank God for His great love.
I thank God for His sacrificial love.
I thank God for His unconditional love.
I thank God for His perfect love.

God's love is unconditional, sacrificial, and without partiality. He gives His love freely and demonstrates it magnificently through the life of His Son. "For God so loved the world that He gave His only begotten Son, that whoever believes in Him should not perish but have everlasting life" (John 3:16 NKJV).

The Apostle Paul expresses God's love as inseparable. "He is convinced that neither death nor life, the present nor the future, nor anything else in all creation, will be able to separate us from the love of God that is in Christ Jesus our Lord, and that God's love is so great that we will never see the end of it or fully know or understand it" (Ephesians 3:19 TLB; Romans 8:37-39 NIV).

God is love, so He can only show love. He is not a heartless Father who punishes us when we miss the mark or turns His face from us when we fall short. God reveals His love through grace, forgiveness, and mercy, and God never changes, so His love does not change. For this reason, let us rejoice and be glad. Let us exalt our Lord and praise His holy name.

Prayerful Praise

Gracious Lord,
Father of Mercy and Goodness,
I praise You for being my God.

Because You love me Lord,
I choose to be loved.
I choose to receive Your love expressed
by Your kindness, goodness, and peace.
I choose to trust in Your love revealed
by Your forgiveness and grace.
I choose to rest in Your love demonstrated
by what Jesus did on the cross.

Gracious Lord,
Father of Mercy and Goodness,
Thank You for giving me Your best.
Thank You for giving me Your love.
In Jesus' name

*I will bless the Lord at
all times; His praise shall
continually be in my mouth.
Psalm 34:1 AMP*

*Let us at all times offer up to God a
sacrifice of praise, which is the fruit of
lips that thankfully acknowledge and
confess and glorify His name.
Hebrews 13:15 AMP*

15

Guard Your Praise

Prophetic Affirmations

I praise the Lord at all times.
I praise the Lord no matter what comes.
I offer to God a sacrifice of praise.
I confess and glorify God's holy name.

Keep speaking words of praise.
Keep acknowledging God for who He is.
Keep empowering yourself by what you say.

I praise the Lord at all times.
I praise the Lord no matter what comes.
I offer to God a sacrifice of praise.
I confess and glorify God's holy name.

Speak the words again.
Be inspired by what you hear!

I praise the Lord at all times.
I praise the Lord no matter what comes.
I offer to God a sacrifice of praise.
I confess and glorify God's holy name.

I once heard a worship leader say, "Whatever you do, guard your praise." Do not let anyone or anything overwhelm you to the point that you cannot find a way to praise God. Praise is an opportunity to honor the Lord and refresh your spirit. When you take your mind off worldly concerns and begin to praise the One who made the world, you usher in the presence and power of God and make room for joyfulness and peace.

God deserves our praise no matter how we feel or what we are experiencing. We should praise Him for who He is and what He has done. We should praise Him because it is what we were born to do. We should praise Him because He is worthy of praise. "Guard your praise." It is God's gift to you.

Prayerful Praise

Heavenly Father,
Glorious and Majestic God,
You are worthy of my praise whether
my life is sunny and bright,
or my days are drenched in sorrow.
Either way, You are God and
You are worthy of exaltation.

Heavenly Father,
Glorious and Majestic God,
Thank You for teaching me that
praising You is a gift and a command.
It is what I was born to do.

Heavenly Father,
Glorious and Majestic God,
As long as I have breath, I will praise You
because You are worthy to be praised.
In Jesus' holy name

God exalted him to the highest place and
gave him the name that is above every
name, that at the name of Jesus every
knee should bow in heaven and on earth
and under the earth, and every tongue
acknowledge that Jesus Christ is Lord,
to the glory of God the Father.
Philippians 2:9-11 NIV

Salvation is found in no one else,
for there is no other name under heaven
given to mankind by which we must be saved.
Acts 4:12 NIV

16

Hallelujah to Jesus

Prophetic Affirmations

I praise Jesus because He is Lord.
I praise Jesus because His name is above all names.
I praise Jesus for the blood He shed for me.
I praise Jesus for giving me life abundantly.

*These words of praise will deepen your
spiritual walk and draw you closer to Jesus.*

I praise Jesus because He is Lord.
I praise Jesus because His name is above all names.
I praise Jesus for the blood He shed for me.
I praise Jesus for giving me life abundantly.

*Repeating these words will bless your
soul and usher you into the presence of God.*

I praise Jesus because He is Lord.
I praise Jesus because His name is above all names.
I praise Jesus for the blood He shed for me.
I praise Jesus for giving me life abundantly.

Hallelujah to Jesus, who is the
Alpha and Omega, Blessed Redeemer,
Bread of Life, and Bright and Morning Star.

Hallelujah to Jesus, who is the
Head of the Church, Image of the
Invisible God, King of kings,
and Lord of lords.

Hallelujah to Jesus, who is the
Light of the World, Living Water,
Prince of Peace, and Rose of Sharon.

Hallelujah to Jesus, who is the
Resurrection and the Life, Savior of
the World, Shepherd of our Souls,
and only Begotten Son of God.

Prayerful Praise

Holy God,
Master of the universe,
Creator and Sustainer of all that exists,
Father of the Lord Jesus Christ,
You are worthy to be praised.

Holy God,
Thank You for Jesus.
Thank You for the blood He shed for me.
Thank You for His sacrifice.
His name is great and greatly to be praised.
His name is above every other name.

Holy God,
Jesus is the name I praise.
To Him be all the glory, majesty,
honor and victory.
Hallelujah and Amen!

*The Lord will open the heavens,
the storehouse of his bounty, to send
rain on your land in season and to
bless all the work of your hands.*
Deuteronomy 28:12 NIV

*Every good and perfect gift is from
above, coming down from the Father
of the heavenly lights, who does
not change like shifting shadows.*
James 1:17 NIV

17

Heavenly Blessings

Prophetic Affirmations

I praise God for blessing the work of my hands.
I praise God for opportunities coming my way.
I praise God for revealing His purpose for my life.
I praise God for everything He does for me.

As you speak these words over and over,
expect feelings of anticipation to rise in your soul.

I praise God for blessing the work of my hands.
I praise God for opportunities coming my way.
I praise God for revealing His purpose for my life.
I praise God for everything He does for me.

When you consistently speak words that agree
with God, you will begin to think like God.
Repetition is the key.

I praise God for blessing the work of my hands.
I praise God for opportunities coming my way.
I praise God for revealing His purpose for my life.
I praise God for everything He does for me.

Sometimes you may feel like you are doing the right thing, but you have not seen the manifestation of God's promises. You see others growing in ministry, starting businesses, publishing books, making financial gains, and getting a significant following on social media. Still, little seems to be happening with you and your endeavors.

We cannot and should not validate ourselves or measure our success by the world's standards, nor judge ourselves by where we think we should be. We can become our own stumbling block when we allow our perceived limitations or resources to dictate our progress. It is better to embrace small beginnings and trust in what God is doing.

I encourage you to stay focused and walk the path ordained for your life because you cannot walk in someone else's shoes or compare your purpose and destiny to theirs. What God has for you is for YOU. He knows what He is doing. Stay on course, do what God tells you to do, and praise Him every step of the way.

Prayerful Praise

Heavenly Father,
You are awesome in all Your ways.
Everything You do is perfect
and worthy of praise.

Thank You for creating me with
unique gifts and talents.
Thank You for giving me thoughts and
desires that line up with Your will.
Thank You for helping me to
believe in myself and in the purpose
You have ordained for me.

Heavenly Father,
Thank You for helping me to stay
on course and to focus on what
You are leading me to do.
May all that I do bring You glory.
In Jesus' holy name, I pray

You alone are the Lord. You made the
heavens, even the highest heavens, and
all their starry host, the earth and all that
is on it, the seas and all that is in them.
You give life to everything, and the
multitudes of heaven worship you.
Nehemiah 9:6 NIV

Let the whole world fear the Lord,
and let everyone stand in awe of him.
For when he spoke, the world began!
It appeared at his command.
Psalm 33:8- 9 NLT

18

He Is Worthy

Prophetic Affirmations

I bless God because He made the heavens.
I bless God because He made the earth.
I bless God because He gives life to everything.
I bless God because He spoke and the world began.

When you talk about blessing God,
you are positioning yourself to
receive from God.

I bless God because He made the heavens.
I bless God because He made the earth.
I bless God because He gives life to everything.
I bless God because He spoke and the world began.

Speak the words again.
Honor God by what you say.

I bless God because He made the heavens.
I bless God because He made the earth.
I bless God because He gives life to everything.
I bless God because He spoke and the world began.

Who established the world?
Who is mightier than all creation?
Who is Omnipotent, Omniscient, and Omnipresent?
The Almighty God who is worthy to be praised.

Who rules the universe?
Who has authority over the galaxies?
Whose splendor radiates throughout the earth?
The Almighty God who is worthy to be praised.

Whose glory echoes from the skies?
Who has dominion over the seas?
Whose voice resounds from the heavens?
The Almighty God who is worthy to be praised.

Who is exalted above the nations?
Who transcends all that exists?
Whose power reigns forever and ever?
The Almighty God who is worthy to be praised.

Prayerful Praise

Almighty God,
Creator of the heavens and the earth,
Ruler over all that exists,
All glory and honor belong to You.

Almighty God,
Maker of the galaxies and the stars,
Sovereign King and Lord of lords,
All splendor and majesty belong to You.

Almighty God,
You are the true and living God.
You reign from the highest heaven.
I exalt You, and I praise You
for You alone are worthy.
Hallelujah and Amen!

Grace, mercy, and peace, which
come from God the Father and from
Jesus Christ, the Son of the Father,
will continue to be with us who
live in truth and love.
2 John 1:3 NLT

Goodness and mercy
and unfailing love shall follow
me all the days of my life.
Psalm 23:6 AMP

19

His Grace and Mercy

Prophetic Affirmations

I praise the Lord for His glorious grace.
I praise the Lord for His infinite mercies.
I praise the Lord for His unfailing love.
I praise the Lord for His everlasting peace.

Repeat the statements over and over.
Let the sound of "glorious grace,
infinite mercies, unfailing love, and
everlasting peace" fill your soul with joy.

I praise the Lord for His glorious grace.
I praise the Lord for His infinite mercies.
I praise the Lord for His unfailing love.
I praise the Lord for His everlasting peace.

Speak the words once more.

I praise the Lord for His glorious grace.
I praise the Lord for His infinite mercies.
I praise the Lord for His unfailing love.
I praise the Lord for His everlasting peace.

*All praise to God, the Father of our
Lord Jesus Christ. It is by his great mercy
that we have been born again, because
God raised Jesus Christ from the dead.
1 Peter 1:3 NLT*

*So we praise God for the glorious
grace he has poured out on us
who belong to his dear Son.
Ephesians 1:6 NLT*

*Praise the Lord! His mercy endures forever.
Psalm 106:1 NKJV*

Prayerful Praise

Heavenly Father,
Mighty and Awesome God,
Holy is Your name.

Thank You for Your peace
that surpasses my understanding.
Thank You for Your grace and mercy
that follow me all the days of my life.

Heavenly Father,
Mighty and Awesome God,
Thank You for loving me.
Thank You for saving me.
In Jesus' mighty name

Jehovah your God is
God of gods and Lord of lords.
He is the great and mighty God.
Deuteronomy 10:17 TLB

O Jehovah, Commander of the
heavenly armies, where is there any
other Mighty One like you?
Faithfulness is your very character.
Psalm 89:8 TLB

20

His Name Is Great

Prophetic Affirmations

I praise God because He is the God of Peace.
I praise God because He is faithful.
I praise God because He is a mighty provider.
I praise God because He is the Lord, my healer.

You can deepen your relationship
with God when you speak words
that magnify His character.

I praise God because He is the God of Peace.
I praise God because He is faithful.
I praise God because He is a mighty provider.
I praise God because He is the Lord, my healer.

Repeat the affirmations.
Strengthen your belief by what you hear.

I praise God because He is the God of Peace.
I praise God because He is faithful.
I praise God because He is a mighty provider.
I praise God because He is the Lord, my healer.

There are many names for God that reveal aspects of His deity. These names were proclaimed by God in the Old Testament as attributes of His character or they were created by man to memorialize divine encounters. For instance, God revealed Himself to the Israelites after they left Egypt as Jehovah Rapha, "I am the Lord, your Healer" (Exodus 15:26)

God gave Ezekiel a vision of the restored city of Jerusalem, and Ezekiel named that place Jehovah-Shammah, "The Lord is There" (Ezekiel 40:1-2, 48:35).

The Angel of the Lord visited Gideon in the city of Ophrah and told Gideon that God would use him to rescue Israel from the Midianites. Gideon built an altar to the Lord at that location and called it Jehovah-Shalom, "The Lord Is Peace" (Judges 6:11-24).

God tested Abraham and told him to take his son Isaac and offer him as a burnt offering. Abraham obeyed, but at the last moment, God intervened and provided a ram for the offering instead of allowing Abraham to sacrifice his son. Abraham called that place Jehovah-Jireh, "The Lord Will Provide" (Genesis 22:1-14).

As you read these examples, I encourage you to choose names that depict God's character and apply them during prayer and praise or to memorialize events that have significant meaning in your life. This method of acknowledging God's presence and power in your life will deepen your relationship with Him, strengthen your prayers, and enhance your worship. Most of all, it will glorify God!

Prayerful Praise

Heavenly Father,
Awesome and True God,
Excellent is Your name.
Wonderful is Your name.
Righteous is Your name.

Your name is above all names.
Your name is great and greatly to be praised.
Your name is glorious and worthy of exaltation.

Heavenly Father,
You are Omniscient and Omnipresent.
You hold all power in Your hands.
There is no one above You or before You.
You reign and rule over everything that exists.

Heavenly Father,
Awesome and True God.
Excellent is Your name in all the earth.
Hallelujah and Amen!

The voice of the Lord is powerful;
the voice of the Lord is majestic.
Psalm 29:4 NIV

His Holy Spirit speaks to us deep in our hearts
and tells us that we really are God's children.
Romans 8:16 TLB

Long ago God spoke in many different
ways to our fathers through the prophets,
in visions, dreams, and even face to face,
telling them little by little about his plans.
Hebrews 1:1 TLB

The whole Bible was given to us
by inspiration from God.
2 Timothy 3:16 TLB

21

I Hear God

Prophetic Affirmations

I praise God for His majestic voice.
I praise God for His gentle whisper.
I praise God for the different ways He speaks.
I praise God because He speaks to me.

The more you talk about hearing God's voice,
the more you will desire to hear Him speak.

I praise God for His majestic voice.
I praise God for His gentle whisper.
I praise God for the different ways He speaks.
I praise God because He speaks to me.

Meditate on these words.
Speak them aloud slowly and consistently.
Increase your faith by what you hear.

I praise God for His majestic voice.
I praise God for His gentle whisper.
I praise God for the different ways He speaks.
I praise God because He speaks to me.

"The Lord thundered from heaven, and the
Most High uttered His voice."
2 Samuel 22:14 NKJV

I heard God speak from the heavens once. To this day, I still remember the booming voice that permeated the night sky. He has also given me messages through prophets, ministers, and other people throughout my life. He has whispered countless words of wisdom to me in the night hours and greeted me with a fresh word in my morning devotions. The Lord has spoken to me in dreams and visions, through wisdom and revelation, and faithfully through the scriptures.

God speaks to all humanity in various ways and times. Job 33:14 says, "God speaks again and again, in one way, or in another." With that in mind, rejoice and expect to hear from God. After all, the Almighty and All-Powerful God, Lord of lords and King of kings, who reigns from the highest heavens and rules over all powers and principalities, desires to communicate with us. Praise His holy name for giving us the ability to hear and understand Him. From every corner of the world, from sunrise to sunset, may He be praised forever and ever!

Prayerful Praise

Heavenly Father,
Sovereign and True God,
I praise Your holy name.

Heavenly Father,
Thank You for creating me
to hear Your voice.
Thank You for giving me
an understanding of what I hear.
Thank You for sensitizing my spiritual
ears to hear the different ways You speak.

Heavenly Father,
Sovereign and True God,
Thank You for speaking to me.
Thank You for teaching me
to hear Your voice.
In Jesus' holy name

*For he has rescued us from
the kingdom of darkness and
transferred us into the Kingdom of
his dear Son, who purchased our
freedom and forgave our sins.
Colossians 1:13-14 NLT*

*I have come as a light to shine
in this dark world, so that all who
put their trust in me will no
longer remain in the dark.
John 12:46 NLT*

22

Light in the Darkness

Prophetic Affirmations

I praise God because He rescued me from
the kingdom of darkness and transferred
me into the Kingdom of His Son.

I praise God because Jesus purchased
my freedom with His blood.

I praise God because He shines His light
of love and mercy into every area of my life.

Speak the affirmations over and over.

I praise God because He rescued me from
the kingdom of darkness and transferred
me into the Kingdom of His Son.

I praise God because Jesus purchased
my freedom with His blood.

I praise God because He shines His light
of love and mercy into every area of my life.

Genesis 1:1-3 NLT says, "In the beginning...the earth was formless and empty, and darkness covered the deep waters. And the Spirit of God was hovering over the surface of the waters. Then God said, 'Let there be light,' and there was light."

Praise God because He has not changed. He is the same today as He was in the beginning. His Spirit continues to hover over the darkness: darkness that resembles fear, anxiety, and despair; darkness that causes oppressive, harmful thoughts and emotional distress; darkness that keeps us in bondage to sin and unbelief; darkness that comes from the devil and spiritual wickedness in high places.

We encounter darkness in many ways, but there is nothing too dark or difficult from which God cannot deliver us. He graciously shines His light of love and mercy upon us to bring us to a place of healing and hope. He hovers over us and speaks to the deep places in our lives. By His Word, miracles happen. By His command, life begins. Praise God, who has all power to dispel the darkness and create light. Praise God because He is worthy to be praised.

Prayerful Praise

Great and Awesome God,
Father of the Lord Jesus Christ,
I bless Your mighty name.

Thank You for bringing me out of the
world and into the light of Your love.
Thank You for rescuing me from
the kingdom of darkness.
Thank You for delivering me from
dark and difficult situations.

Great and Awesome God,
Thank You for hovering over me
and shining Your glorious light
into the dark areas of my soul.
Thank You for all that You do for me.
In Jesus' holy name, I pray

Praise be to the name of God for ever
and ever; wisdom and power are his.
Daniel 2:20 NIV

Praise him for his acts of power;
praise him for his surpassing greatness.
Psalm 150:2 NIV

Praise the Lord, all you nations.
Praise him, all you people of the earth.
For his unfailing love for us is powerful;
the Lord's faithfulness endures forever.
Psalm 117:1-2 NLT

23

Love and Faithfulness

Prophetic Affirmations

I praise God for His unfailing love.
I praise God for His acts of power.
I praise God for His surpassing greatness.
I praise God for His eternal faithfulness.

*Repeating these words will strengthen
your soul and gladden your heart.*

I praise God for His unfailing love.
I praise God for His acts of power.
I praise God for His surpassing greatness.
I praise God for His eternal faithfulness.

*Continue to speak these words aloud.
Use your voice to bless yourself.
Rejoice in what you hear.*

I praise God for His unfailing love.
I praise God for His acts of power.
I praise God for His surpassing greatness.
I praise God for His eternal faithfulness.

God's blessings are inexhaustible.
His faithfulness is eternal.
His favor is for a lifetime.
His gifts are irrevocable.
His goodness is forever.
His compassion is unchanging.
His grace is immeasurable.
His joy is abiding.
His love is unfailing.
His mercies are endless.
His peace is perfect.
His power is infinite.
His Word is everlasting.

All glory and honor to God, for He is the
Almighty God, who remains faithful to
His children, and He does not change!

Prayerful Praise

Sovereign Lord and Savior,
Every morning I will praise You.
In the evening, I will praise You again.

I praise You for Your goodness and
Your surpassing greatness.
I praise You for Your lovingkindness
and Your faithfulness.
I praise You for Your countless mercies
and Your never-ending grace.

Sovereign Lord and Savior,
Accept my praise, oh God.
Accept the sacrifice of my heart.
Accept the gratitude in my soul.
In the mighty name of Jesus,
I praise You, and I exalt Your holy name.

*Then God said, "Let the water beneath
the sky be gathered into oceans so that the
dry land will emerge." And so it was.
Then God named the dry land "earth," and
the water "seas." And God was pleased.*
Genesis 1:9-10 TLB

*The sea is His, for He made it [by
His command]; and His hands
formed the dry land.*
Psalm 95:5 AMP

24

Mightier Than the Seas

Prophetic Affirmations

I praise God because He made the earth.
I praise God because He put the oceans in place.
I praise God because He set the limits of the seas.
I praise God because He has authority over everything.

The more you speak words of praise,
the more of God's glory you will experience.
Keep speaking. Bless yourself by what you say.

I praise God because He made the earth.
I praise God because He put the oceans in place.
I praise God because He set the limits of the seas.
I praise God because He has authority over everything.

Say the words again.
Remember to speak aloud.

I praise God because He made the earth.
I praise God because He put the oceans in place.
I praise God because He set the limits of the seas.
I praise God because He has authority over everything.

God is mightier than the rushing seas.
His voice is louder than thunderous waters.
He alone reigns over the oceans and the streams.
God has authority over everything.

The seas parted at God's holy command.
The rivers stopped flowing when He sent His Word.
By His great power, water flowed from a rock.
God has authority over everything.

God set boundaries for the depths of the oceans.
By His command, the seas know how far to go.
He monitors the length and width of every river.
God has authority over everything.

*He does whatever pleases him throughout all of
heaven and earth and in the deepest seas.
Psalm 135:6 TLB*

Prayerful Praise

Mighty God,
Great and Glorious Lord,
Creator of the heavens and the earth,
You are worthy of the highest praise.

Mighty God,
There is none like You.
There is none above You or before You.
You are the Omnipotent, Omniscient God.
By Your will, You established the world.
By Your command all things exist.
You are the source of every living thing.

Mighty God,
Great and Glorious Lord,
I bless Your holy name.
Hallelujah and Amen!

God saw all that he had made, and it
was very good. And there was evening,
and there was morning—the sixth day.
Genesis 1:31 NIV

This is the day the Lord has made.
We will rejoice and be glad in it.
Psalm 118:24 NLT

25

Morning Worship

Prophetic Affirmations

I bless the Lord for the morning.
I lift my voice and offer praise to my Father.
I speak words of gratitude to the Lord.
I thank God for blessing me with another day.

*Keep saying what you do until you
do what you say. Use your voice
to empower yourself.*

I bless the Lord for the morning.
I lift my voice and offer praise to my Father.
I speak words of gratitude to the Lord.
I thank God for blessing me with another day.

*Repeat the words once more. Use your
voice to develop the discipline of praise.*

I bless the Lord for the morning.
I lift my voice and offer praise to my Father.
I speak words of gratitude to the Lord.
I thank God for blessing me with another day.

When you wake up in the morning,
Do you give a shout-out to God?
Do you say "hallelujah" to the Lord?
Do you stop to thank Jesus for another day?

When you wake up in the morning,
Do you speak words of gratitude to God?
Do you exalt His great name?
Do you bless Him for His wondrous works?

When you wake up in the morning,
Do you remind yourself of God's promises?
Do you acknowledge Him for His goodness?
Do you embrace the purpose He has for you?

When you wake up in the morning,
Do you recognize that the
morning is God's gift to you?

Prayerful Praise

Most Holy God,
Creator of the world,
I exalt Your great name.

Most Holy God,
You alone cause the sun to rise.
You call each day into existence and
determine when the morning begins.
Each day happens because of You.

Most Holy God,
I welcome the gift of today.
I embrace it with gratitude and hope.
I rejoice because this is the day
that You have made.
All glory and honor belong to You.
In Jesus' holy name

Now may the Lord of peace
Himself grant you His peace
at all times and in every way.
2 Thessalonians 3:16 AMP

And the peace of God, which
transcends all understanding,
will guard your hearts and your
minds in Christ Jesus.
Philippians 4:7 NIV

The Lord blesses his people with peace.
Psalm 29:11 NIV

26

Perfect Peace

Prophetic Affirmations

I thank God for blessing me with peace.
I thank God for keeping me calm.
I thank God because His peace guards my heart.
I thank God because His peace is perfect.

*Speaking words of peace will help
keep your mind at ease.*

I thank God for blessing me with peace.
I thank God for keeping me calm.
I thank God because His peace guards my heart.
I thank God because His peace is perfect.

*Say the words aloud. Pause after each
statement. Then close your eyes and rest
in the goodness of God's perfect peace.*

I thank God for blessing me with peace.
I thank God for keeping me calm.
I thank God because His peace guards my heart.
I thank God because His peace is perfect.

A friend once asked me, "What is the point of peace if you still have the problem." I responded, "The point is that you will always have problems, but God's peace will give you a deep calm in your soul, a feeling of wholeness, and a belief that the God of heaven and earth is with you, sustaining you, comforting you, and working all things for your good."

Peace is not the absence of anxiety, affliction, or sorrow; it is the presence of Jesus reigning in our souls, regardless of the circumstance. Peace is not contingent on the solution or elimination of a problem. Peace prevails through pain and sorrow and carries you through heartbreak until you can experience joy. It is present in hard times, discord, and tragedy. It keeps us steady when we feel like giving up and lifts our souls when we are desperate and discouraged.

God's peace is supernatural, and it transcends human understanding. But we have to make room for His peace by acknowledging God, exalting His sovereignty over our troubles, praying instead of worrying, praising instead of complaining, and believing that God is our hope and our help.

Give the Lord your anxieties and discomforts and exchange them for His perfect peace. His peace will "calm you in every circumstance and give you courage and strength for every challenge" (John 14:27 AMP).

Prayerful Praise

Heavenly Father,
Most High God,
Glorious Lord and God of Peace,
I praise Your holy name.

Heavenly Father,
Please help me to surrender all my
concerns to You, to let go of everything
that causes me to be anxious or unsettled
that I may experience Your perfect peace.

Heavenly Father,
Most High God,
Thank You for Your peace.
Thank You for keeping me calm.
Thank You for caring about me.
In Jesus' holy name

Let all that I am praise the Lord;
with my whole heart, I will praise
His holy name. May I never forget
the good things he does for me.
Psalm 103:1-2 NLT

Praise the Lord; praise God our savior!
For each day he carries us in his arms.
Psalm 68:19 NLT

27

Praise God!

Prophetic Affirmations

I praise God for His kindness.
I praise God for His strength.
I praise God because He provides for my needs.
I praise God for the things He does for me.

Keep blessing God with your words.
Keep encouraging yourself by what you say.

I praise God for His kindness.
I praise God for His strength.
I praise God because He provides for my needs.
I praise God for the things He does for me.

Speak the words again aloud.
Keep talking about God's goodness.
Increase your faith by what you hear.

I praise God for His kindness.
I praise God for His strength.
I praise God because He provides for my needs.
I praise God for the things He does for me.

Praise God when you are on the mountain top.
Praise God when you are in the valley deep.
Praise God in every situation, whether good or bad.
Praise God because He is worthy to be praised.

Praise God when days are difficult.
Praise God when everything seems at ease.
Praise God if you are destitute or living in plenty.
Praise God because He is worthy to be praised.

Praise God when you are smiling and feeling free.
Praise God when there is trouble on every side.
Praise God if you are up or down in the dumps.
Praise God because He is worthy to be praised.

Praise God when times are cloudy and confusing.
Praise God during seasons of joy and peace.
Praise God when you feel purposeful or just existing.
Praise God because He is worthy to be praised.

Prayerful Praise

Heavenly Father,
God of all Might and Mercy,
You are worthy of the highest praise.

Heavenly Father,
Sometimes life is going great,
no pressing situations, trauma, drama,
or strife. But then there are times when
my heart is heavy, and not giving into
my discontent is a challenge.
Please help me to remember that
these are the times to come to You
and find rest for my soul.

Heavenly Father,
Thank You for being my hope and my help.
Thank You for being everything I need.
In Jesus' glorious name

So let us come boldly to the throne of
our gracious God. There we will receive
his mercy, and we will find grace to
help us when we need it most.
Hebrews 4:16 NLT

Surely God is my help; the Lord
is the one who sustains me.
Psalm 54:4 NIV

28

Praising Through the Pain

Prophetic Affirmations

I bless the Lord when my heart is hurting.
I bless the Lord when I am in pain.
I bless the Lord when my body is aching.
I bless the Lord when times are hard.

*Rehearsing words of praise will help
you to maintain a spirit of praise and a
spirit of praise will keep you focused on God!*

I bless the Lord when my heart is hurting.
I bless the Lord when I am in pain.
I bless the Lord when my body is aching.
I bless the Lord when times are hard.

*Repeat the words. Encourage yourself
by the words of your mouth.*

I bless the Lord when my heart is hurting.
I bless the Lord when I am in pain.
I bless the Lord when my body is aching.
I bless the Lord when times are hard.

When we praise God, we are
exalting the One who understands
the complexity of our pain,
the afflictions of our soul,
and the physical hurt we bear.

When we praise God, we are
honoring the One who
rescues us from troubles,
delivers us from our enemies,
and gives us hope for better days.

When we praise God, we are
worshiping the One who is awesome
and mighty, faithful and true,
and worthy of our praise.

Prayerful Praise

Heavenly Father,
There are not enough words to convey
the gratitude I feel in my heart for all
that You have done and will do for me.

I repent for the times I turned to the
world for answers, or found myself
anxious and worried instead of
bringing my concerns to You.

Heavenly Father,
Thank You for Your lovingkindness.
You are everything that I need.
You are my comforter and my deliverer.
You are my healer, my helper, and my hope.
To You, I give my praise.
In Jesus' name

The Lord your God in your midst,
The Mighty One, will save;
He will rejoice over you with gladness,
He will quiet you with His love,
He will rejoice over you with singing.
Zephaniah 3:17 NKJV

He has given me a new song to sing,
a hymn of praise to our God.
Psalm 40:3 NLT

29

Sing A New Song

Prophetic Affirmations

I bless the Lord because He sings over me.
I bless the Lord for rejoicing over me with gladness.
I bless the Lord for giving me a song of praise.
I bless the Lord for giving me a new song to sing.

*The words you speak will help you
grow closer to God. The words you
speak will increase your faith.*

I bless the Lord because He sings over me.
I bless the Lord for rejoicing over me with gladness.
I bless the Lord for giving me a song of praise.
I bless the Lord for giving me a new song to sing.

*Repeat the words.
There is power in what you say.*

I bless the Lord because He sings over me.
I bless the Lord for rejoicing over me with gladness.
I bless the Lord for giving me a song of praise.
I bless the Lord for giving me a new song to sing.

Have you ever awakened with a song in your heart, started humming a tune you did not know, singing a hymn you had not heard in years, or maybe you began to pray or read scriptures, but only singing came forth? These are times ordained by God, so I encourage you to surrender to what He is doing. He is giving you a song to sing unto Him, a message through the lyrics, a glorious way to set the atmosphere for your day, or leading you into a time of intimacy with Him.

I love when this happens because when God gives us songs, He is rejoicing over us. He blesses us with songs of love, joy, deliverance, and peace, and He delights in us when we sing these songs back to Him in worship and praise.

The more you yield to the Holy Spirit in this way, the more you will experience God's presence in your life. As you move through your day, embrace the songs as they resonate in your soul. Even if you are not singing aloud, you may still hear the melody in your heart. Enjoy these moments and thank the Lord for the creative ways He draws us close to Him. And be attentive because God always gives us songs, not just at random moments. There is a song in your heart right now. Quiet yourself, listen for it, and begin to sing it aloud.

How sweet is our God that He desires to sing to us, through us, and over us. He graciously gives us messages through songs that strengthen, inspire, and prepare us for our day. How great is our God! How mighty is our Lord! He is forever worthy of our worship, gratitude, and praise!

Prayerful Praise

Great and Mighty God,
You are worthy of the highest praise.
There is no one as gracious or faithful as You.
There is no one as loving or kind as You.
There is no one as holy as You.

Great and Mighty God,
There are no words to express the
magnitude and gratitude of knowing that
the Creator of all that exists sings over
me and rejoices over me with gladness.

Thank You for the songs You put in my heart.
Thank You for Your words of
encouragement, messages of love,
and songs of deliverance.

Great and Mighty God,
You are worthy of the highest praise.
Hallelujah and Amen!

I will give thanks and praise You,
O Lord my God, with all my heart; and
will glorify Your name forevermore.
Psalm 86:12 AMP

All day long I'll praise and honor you,
O God, for all that you have done for me.
Psalm 71:8 TLB

30

Take Time to Praise

Prophetic Affirmations

I begin my day by giving thanks to God.
I pause to rejoice in the Lord my Savior.
I take time to praise the God of the heavens.
I take time to praise the Lord my God.

Keep talking about what you should be doing.
Change your habits by what you say.

I begin my day by giving thanks to God.
I pause to rejoice in the Lord my Savior.
I take time to praise the God of the heavens.
I take time to praise the Lord my God.

Keep speaking these affirmations.
Repetition is a catalyst for change.

I begin my day by giving thanks to God.
I pause to rejoice in the Lord my Savior.
I take time to praise the God of the heavens.
I take time to praise the Lord my God.

Running here and there,
Going to and fro,
Doing this and that,
Planning and preparing,
Making schedules, setting goals,
Getting up early, going to bed late,
Over and over again, moving, doing, going.

But all in vain if we have not stopped to spend
time with our Creator, to worship the giver of time,
and to praise the God of the heavens.

So, when we run, let us pause.
When we go, let us stop.
In all our busyness, let us take time to rest.
And before we begin, let us greet our God.

Prayerful Praise

Heavenly Father,
Sovereign Lord and Sustainer of Life,
You hold time and eternity in Your hands.
Every moment is a gift from You.

Heavenly Father,
Every day comes with a multitude of
responsibilities, routines, and personal ventures,
but none of these things are more important
than spending time with You.

Please help me to discipline myself
to make You the first part of my day,
and to acknowledge You in all my ways.

Heavenly Father,
May all that I do bring you glory.
In Jesus' holy name

The Lord is my strength and my song,
And He has become my salvation;
This is my God, and I will praise Him.
Exodus 15:2 AMP

Praise be to the God and Father
of our Lord Jesus Christ, the Father of
compassion and the God of all comfort.
2 Corinthians 1:3 NIV

31

Thanksgiving Day

Prophetic Affirmations

I praise the Lord for His comfort and grace.
I praise the Lord for His strength and peace.
I praise the Lord for His love and compassion.
I praise the Lord because He cares about me.

Speak faith-filled words during times of happiness so that you may be stronger during seasons of sadness.

I praise the Lord for His comfort and grace.
I praise the Lord for His strength and peace.
I praise the Lord for His love and compassion.
I praise the Lord because He cares about me.

Say the words with courage and conviction. Encourage your heart by what you hear.

I praise the Lord for His comfort and grace.
I praise the Lord for His strength and peace.
I praise the Lord for His love and compassion.
I praise the Lord because He cares about me.

On Thanksgiving Day, November 26, 2020, I had just turned on some music to create an atmosphere of praise when I received a phone call that my brother, Steve, had passed away. Sorrow and shock gripped my family, and the Thanksgiving holiday grew more somber by the moment. We had many questions, but no explanation was good enough because the finality of physical life was still the same.

We may never have the answers we want; even if we did, none of them would take away our sorrow or bring my brother back. The truth remains that Steve is alive and well in the presence of the Lord, and a reunion in Christ is inevitable. Furthermore, God has not changed. He is faithful to heal, deliver, comfort, and strengthen His beloved in their brokenness.

With shattered hearts and tears of sadness, we still praised God, for there is no hope, peace, comfort, or promise of eternal life without God, the Father of our Lord Jesus Christ. In Him, we have everything we need. To God be all the glory!

Prayerful Praise

God of all Comfort,
Father of all Grace,
Faithful and True God,
I bless Your majestic name.

God of all Comfort,
Please strengthen those who woke
up today to the loneliness of grief.
Comfort those whose hearts are
overwhelmed with sorrow and bless
all those who are in seasons of sadness.
May we all remain hopeful and not
despair from the hardships of this life.

God of all Comfort,
Thank You for caring about me.
Thank You for being everything I need.
In Jesus' holy name, I pray

The angel replied, "The Holy Spirit
will come upon you, and the power of
the Most High will overshadow you.
So the baby to be born will be holy,
and he will be called the Son of God."
Luke 1:35 NLT

For it is my Father's will
that all who see his Son and believe
in him should have eternal life.
John 6:40 NLT

32

The Anointed King

Prophetic Affirmations

I praise Jesus because He is my Lord and Savior.
I praise Jesus for sacrificing His life for me.
I praise Jesus for redeeming my soul.
I praise Jesus for giving me a divine destiny.

In Christ, you have a divine destiny.
Speak this truth often and be
strengthened by what you hear.

I praise Jesus because He is my Lord and Savior.
I praise Jesus for sacrificing His life for me.
I praise Jesus for redeeming my soul.
I praise Jesus for giving me a divine destiny.

Say the affirmations once more.
Focus on the words "I praise Jesus."

I praise Jesus because He is my Lord and Savior.
I praise Jesus for sacrificing His life for me.
I praise Jesus for redeeming my soul.
I praise Jesus for giving me a divine destiny.

Glory to the newborn King.
Glory to the One who forever reigns.
Hallelujah, now the world can sing.
"Hallelujah, we are no longer in chains."

Look and see what the Lord has done.
The bells of freedom have finally rung.
God sent Jesus; our Savior has come.
Shout to the hilltops,
"Come and see the Anointed One."

Send the message around the earth.
There has indeed been a virgin birth.
The promised One has arrived; sound the alert.
"Jesus has come to remove the curse."

The heavens burst forth with resounding praise,
As the people rejoice and stand amazed.
"Hallelujah, hallelujah to the newborn King.
Always and forever, our Redeemer reigns."

Prayerful Praise

All-Wise and Perfect God,
Master of the universe,
Holy and Awesome is Your name.

All-Wise and Perfect God,
Thank You for Your miraculous plan
to bring Your Son from heaven to earth.
Thank You for our precious Redeemer.
Thank You for the Anointed One.
Thank You for Jesus.

All-Wise and Perfect God,
Master of the universe,
Blessed be Your holy name.
Hallelujah and Amen!

But the Helper (Comforter, Advocate,
Intercessor—Counselor, Strengthener,
Standby), the Holy Spirit, whom the Father
will send in My name [in My place, to
represent Me and act on My behalf], He will
teach you all things. And He will help you
remember everything that I have told you.
John 14:26 AMP

Then Peter said to them, "Repent,
and let every one of you be baptized
in the name of Jesus Christ for the
remission of sins; and you shall
receive the gift of the Holy Spirit."
Acts 2:38 NKJV

33

The Holy Spirit

Prophetic Affirmations

I bless the Holy Spirit because He is a gift from God.
I bless the Holy Spirit because He teaches me all things.
I bless the Holy Spirit because He is always with me.
I bless the Holy Spirit because He is the Spirit of God.

Keep speaking about the Holy Spirit.
Keep talking about God.

I bless the Holy Spirit because He is a gift from God.
I bless the Holy Spirit because He teaches me all things.
I bless the Holy Spirit because He is always with me.
I bless the Holy Spirit because He is the Spirit of God.

Speak the affirmations over and over until you
believe what you say. Allow the words to bless
your heart and fill your soul with joy.

I bless the Holy Spirit because He is a gift from God.
I bless the Holy Spirit because He teaches me all things.
I bless the Holy Spirit because He is always with me.
I bless the Holy Spirit because He is the Spirit of God.

The Holy Spirit is the Spirit of God living in you.
He is majestic, eternal, and all-knowing.
He is omnipresent, excellent, and just.

The Holy Spirit is the glory of God living in you.
He is omnipotent, all-wise, and sovereign.
He is self-existent, perfect, and complete.

The Holy Spirit is the presence of God living in you.
He is the Comforter, Advocate and Helper.
He is the Teacher and Revealer of divine truth.
The Holy Spirit is God's gift to you.

He (the Holy Spirit) remains with you
continually and will be in you.
John 14:17 AMP

Prayerful Praise

Holy Lord, Omnipotent Father,
From everlasting to everlasting,
You are God.

I cannot thank You enough for the
the Holy Spirit who lives in me,
talks with me, and reminds me
that I belong to You.

I cannot thank You enough for the
Holy Spirit who gives me insight
into spiritual things, teaches me
about Jesus, and helps me to pray.

Holy Lord, Omnipotent Father,
Thank You for Your gift.
Thank You for the Holy Spirit.
In Jesus' mighty name

In Christ there is all
of God in a human body.
Colossians 2:9 TLB

The Lord is the Spirit.
2 Corinthians 3:17 NLT

Go ye therefore, and teach all nations,
baptizing them in the name of the Father,
and of the Son, and of the Holy Ghost.
Matthew 28:18-19 KJV

34

The Holy Trinity

Prophetic Affirmations

I exalt God, who is the Almighty Father.
I exalt Jesus, who is the Son of God.
I exalt the Holy Ghost, who is the Spirit of God.
I exalt the Holy Trinity.

How beautiful it is to declare words
of praise about the divine nature of God.

I exalt God, who is the Almighty Father.
I exalt Jesus, who is the Son of God.
I exalt the Holy Ghost, who is the Spirit of God.
I exalt the Holy Trinity.

These are powerful words that will
usher you into the presence of God.
Say them once more.

I exalt God, who is the Almighty Father.
I exalt Jesus, who is the Son of God.
I exalt the Holy Ghost, who is the Spirit of God.
I exalt the Holy Trinity.

Praise God from whom all blessings flow.
Praise Father, Son, and Holy Ghost.
Their glory reigns throughout eternity.
They are one, but they are three.
Hallelujah to the Holy Trinity.

Alpha and Omega, First and the Last,
Almighty, All-Powerful, ruling to the end.
Sovereign, Supreme, Majestic, and Just,
They are one, but they are three.
Hallelujah to the Holy Trinity.

He is my Lord; He is my God.
He is my Father; He is my friend.
He is my rock, and He is my savior.
He is one, but He is three.
Hallelujah to the Holy Trinity.

Prayerful Praise

Mighty God,
Self-Sufficient, Self-Existent God,
You are the First and the Last,
Beginning and the End,
and I praise Your holy name.

Mighty God,
In my finite mind, I am incapable
of understanding the Trinity, but I
believe by faith that You are one,
Father, Son, and Holy Ghost.

Mighty God,
Father of the Lord Jesus Christ,
All praise, glory, and honor
belong to You and You alone.
Hallelujah and Amen!

Yet there is one ray of hope:
His compassion never ends. It is only
the Lord's mercies that have kept us
from complete destruction. Great is
his faithfulness; his loving-kindness
begins afresh each day.
Lamentations 3:21-23 TLB

God is our refuge and strength,
an ever-present help in trouble.
The Lord Almighty is with us;
the God of Jacob is our fortress.
Psalm 46:1, 7 NIV

35

The Lord Our Refuge

Prophetic Affirmations

I bless God because He is all-powerful.
I bless God because He is my place of safety.
I bless God because He is always ready to help.
I bless God for the plans He has for me.

Speak the affirmations again aloud.
Encourage yourself by what you hear.
Repetition is the key.

I bless God because He is all-powerful.
I bless God because He is my place of safety.
I bless God because He is always ready to help.
I bless God for the plans He has for me.

Honor God with your words of praise.
Deepen your belief by what you say.

I bless God because He is all-powerful.
I bless God because He is my place of safety.
I bless God because He is always ready to help.
I bless God for the plans He has for me.

2020 was a horrendous year, primarily due to the Coronavirus pandemic. Millions were affected, and the number of deaths was staggering. Restrictions on human touch and lack of socialization were unprecedented. Many businesses, including restaurants, schools, churches, gyms, and more, had to close, interrupting normal activities and increasing unemployment. Fear, isolation, depression, anxiety, pain, and despair had gripped people worldwide. The weight of sorrow was monumental, and life as we knew it had changed.

Many people said, "2020 is a terrible year; we cannot wait until 2021." But it does not matter what the year is because pandemics, wars, riots, famines, injustices, death, and sorrow can occur anytime and wreak havoc on our lives. The good news is that God is still in control, and His power is greater than anything. Moreover, He is the One who will comfort us in difficult times and give us hope for a better future. He is the One who will deliver us from the adversities of this world and give us a life where there is "no more death or mourning or crying or pain" (Revelation 21:4). Therefore, praise God regardless of the times or circumstances. He alone is worthy, every day and all day, this year and the next.

Prayerful Praise

Great and Awesome God,
All-Powerful, Omnipresent Father,
I bless Your holy name.

There is trouble everywhere.
Tragedy strikes at a moment's notice.
Everything changes, and one challenge
after another comes before us.

Great and Awesome God,
I bless You because You never change.
I bless You because nothing is too hard for You.
I bless You for Your great mercies.
I bless You because You always take care of me.

Great and Awesome God,
I bless Your holy name.
Hallelujah and Amen!

*Your unfailing love, O Lord, is as
vast as the heavens; your faithfulness
reaches beyond the clouds. Your
righteousness is like the mighty
mountains, your justice like
the ocean depths. You care for
people and animals alike, O Lord.
How precious is your unfailing
love, O God. All humanity finds
shelter in the shadow of your wings.
Psalm 36:5-7 NLT*

36

Unfailing Love

Prophetic Affirmations

I bless God for His unfailing love.
I bless God for His amazing faithfulness.
I bless God for the glory of His presence.
I bless God because He cares for me.

Talk about blessing God until
you feel His loving presence.

I bless God for His unfailing love.
I bless God for His amazing faithfulness.
I bless God for the glory of His presence.
I bless God because He cares for me.

Say the words again.
Speak slowly and emphasize
the words "I bless God."

I bless God for His unfailing love.
I bless God for His amazing faithfulness.
I bless God for the glory of His presence.
I bless God because He cares for me.

Pause and breathe in the goodness of God.
Take a moment to acknowledge His presence.
Spend time inhaling the fragrance of His
Spirit and fill yourself with His love.

Stand still and bask in God's glory.
Find shelter in the shadow of His wings.
Wait quietly and reflect on His faithfulness
and for your Father to express His great love.

*We know how much God loves us because we
have felt his love and because we believe him
when he tells us that he loves us dearly.*
1 John 4:16 TLB

Prayerful Praise

Dear Lord,
How beautiful it is to bask in Your
presence, to rest in Your unfailing love,
and to know that the God of all creation
loves me unconditionally and sacrificially.

What a blessing it is to realize that
no matter what happens in life, I can
hide in the shadow of Your wings.
Your love covers me and protects me.

Dear Lord,
Thank You for Your amazing faithfulness.
Thank You for Your unfailing love.
In Jesus' holy name, I pray

You will not have to fight this battle.
Take up your positions; stand firm and
see the deliverance the Lord will give you.
2 Chronicles 20:17 NIV

For the Lord your God is the One who
goes with you to fight for you against
your enemies to give you victory.
Deuteronomy 20:4 NIV

37

Victory Begins With Praise

Prophetic Affirmations

I bless the Lord because He fights my battles.
I bless the Lord because He does great things.
I bless the Lord because He causes me to succeed.
I bless the Lord because He gives me the victory.

*When you speak about the greatness of God,
you are positioning yourself to experience
the greatness of God.*

I bless the Lord because He fights my battles.
I bless the Lord because He does great things.
I bless the Lord because He causes me to succeed.
I bless the Lord because He gives me the victory.

*Keep speaking.
God is listening to what you say.*

I bless the Lord because He fights my battles.
I bless the Lord because He does great things.
I bless the Lord because He causes me to succeed.
I bless the Lord because He gives me the victory.

Here, in part, is the story of Jehoshaphat. During his reign as King of Judah, Jehoshaphat received a message that a vast army (Ammonites, Moabites, and people from Mount Seir) were coming to wage war against him.

Jehoshaphat called the people to fast and implore God for direction, and God answered them through Jahaziel, the prophet. He told Jehoshaphat to confront his enemies because God would fight for the people of Judah and Jerusalem. Jehoshaphat obeyed, and the following day the people began to march against their enemies, with the praise team at the head of the army. When the people began to praise and sing unto the Lord, God moved on their behalf. He caused the men of Ammon, Moab, and Mount Seir to fight against themselves, so when Jehoshaphat and his army arrived, those who had come up against him had killed each other off. (2 Chronicles 20)

What an example of the mighty power of praise. When our praises go up and touch heaven's ears, the glorious power of God comes down and touches the lives of men. God is faithful to fight your battles, and He will cause you to win. Hallelujah. Praise His holy name!

Prayerful Praise

God of all Might and Power,
You are great and greatly to be praised.
Glory to Your holy name.

Thank You for causing me to triumph
in every battle, every struggle,
and every difficulty I face.
Thank You for teaching me how to
rest in Your strength and to praise
You even before the test is over.
Thank You for fighting my battles.
Thank You for giving me the victory.

God of all Might and Power,
Thank You for causing me to triumph
in every area of my life.
Thank You for caring about me.
In the precious and holy name of Jesus,
I thank You, and I praise You.

*For the Spirit of God has
made me, and the breath of the
Almighty gives me life.
Job 33:4 NLT*

*Before the mountains were born
or before You had given birth to
the earth and the world, even
from everlasting to everlasting,
You are [the eternal] God.
Psalm 90:2 AMP*

38

Without God

Prophetic Affirmations

I exalt God because He made me.
I exalt God because He gave me life.
I exalt God as the Lord God Almighty.
I exalt God as the Creator of all that exists.

Speak these words aloud.
You will be blessed by what you hear
while honoring God by what you say!

I exalt God because He made me.
I exalt God because He gave me life.
I exalt God as the Lord God Almighty.
I exalt God as the Creator of all that exists.

Repeat the words once more.
Let your soul be delighted in what you say.

I exalt God because He made me.
I exalt God because He gave me life.
I exalt God as the Lord God Almighty.
I exalt God as the Creator of all that exists.

Without God, there would be no sunrise.
Without God, the stars would never shine.
Without God, there would be no rainbows in the sky.
Without God, there would be neither birds nor butterflies.

Without God, the rivers would stop flowing.
Without God, there would be no fish to fill the seas.
Without God, there would be no lofty mountains.
Without God, there would be no rustling in the trees.

Without God, there would be no day or night.
Without God, there would be no summer breeze.
Without God, there would be no flowers in the fields.
Without God, there would be no air to breathe.

Without God, there would be no hope.
Without God, there would be no saving grace.
Without God, there would be no peace to pursue.
Without God, there would be no me nor you.

Prayerful Praise

Most High God,
You are the source of life.
You established the earth
and formed the heavens.

Most High God,
You gave purpose and order to the world.
You put everything in place according
to Your wisdom, and You
uphold all things by Your power.

Most High God,
I exalt You for Your mighty works.
All glory belongs to You.
In Jesus' name

Suddenly, the angel was joined by a vast
host of others—the armies of heaven—
praising God and saying, "Glory to God
in highest heaven, and peace on earth
to those with whom God is pleased."
Luke 2:13-14 NLT

Praise him, all his angels;
praise him, all his heavenly hosts.
Psalm 148:2 NIV

39

Worship Like the Angels

Prophetic Affirmations

I praise the Lord for His creation.
I praise the Lord for His heavenly hosts.
I praise the Lord because He is holy.
I praise the Lord because He is God.

What a privilege it is to praise God.
What an honor it is to bless the Lord.
Keep speaking. Rejoice in what you hear.

I praise the Lord for His creation.
I praise the Lord for His heavenly hosts.
I praise the Lord because He is holy.
I praise the Lord because He is God.

Speak the words over and over.
Be blessed by what you say.

I praise the Lord for His creation.
I praise the Lord for His heavenly hosts.
I praise the Lord because He is holy.
I praise the Lord because He is God.

Then I looked and heard the voice of many angels,
numbering thousands upon thousands, and ten
thousand times ten thousand. They encircled the
throne and the living creatures and the elders.
In a loud voice they were saying:
"Worthy is the Lamb, who was slain, to
receive power and wealth and wisdom and
strength and honor and glory and praise!"
Revelation 5:11-12 NIV

God created us to worship like the angels,
to come boldly before His throne of grace,
and lift our voices in continual praise.
GLORY to His holy name!

Prayerful Praise

Holy Father,
Omnipotent, Omnipresent
and Omniscience God,
Hallelujah to Your excellent name.

Holy Father,
Rain down Your Spirit.
Fill me with Your joy and peace.
Let me feel Your loving presence.

Holy Father,
Faithful and True God,
I pray to worship like the angels.
I pray to please You with my praise.
I pray to give You all the glory.
In Jesus' majestic name

Enter his gates with thanksgiving
and his courts with praise; give thanks
to him and praise his name. For the
Lord is good and his love endures
forever; his faithfulness continues
through all generations.
Psalm 100:4-5 NIV

For great is the Lord and
most worthy of praise.
1 Chronicles 16:25 NIV

40

Worthy of My Praise

Prophetic Affirmations

I praise God for blessing me abundantly.
I praise God for every blessing in heaven.
I praise God for everything He has done for me.
I praise God because He is worthy of my praise.

*The more you speak words of praise the
more grateful you will become.*

I praise God for blessing me abundantly.
I praise God for every blessing in heaven.
I praise God for everything He has done for me.
I praise God because He is worthy of my praise.

*Repeat the affirmations over and over until
the words fill your heart with happiness.
Be inspired by what YOU say.*

I praise God for blessing me abundantly.
I praise God for every blessing in heaven.
I praise God for everything He has done for me.
I praise God because He is worthy of my praise.

God is worthy of our praise!

He loves us,
Accepts us in Christ,
Forgives our sins,
Helps us to live righteously,
Keeps us from falling,
Fills us with hope,
Gives us His peace.

He fights our battles,
Rescues us from troubles,
Sends His angels to protect us,
Shows us tender mercies,
Surrounds us with favor,
Secures our future in Christ,
Promises life eternally.

And I could go on and on because
"God has blessed us with every blessing in
heaven because we belong to Christ."
Ephesians 1:3 TLB

Prayerful Praise

Lord of lords and King of kings,
God and Father of the Lord Jesus Christ,
Creator and Sustainer of the heavens,
You are worthy of the highest praise.

Lord of lords and King of kings,
You bless me with strength and hope.
You bless me with joy and peace.
You bless me with mercy and grace.
You bless me with kindness and love.
Thank You for blessing me.

Lord of lords and King of kings,
Thank You for blessing me with every
blessing in heaven because I belong to Christ.
Thank You for blessing me abundantly.
In Jesus' holy name

For more information on "Prophetic Affirmations"
and to purchase additional copies of Ms. Slade's
works visit her official website
@www.propheticaffirmations.com

Possess the Purpose
(31-day devotional on the Book of Ephesians)

Live in the Moment
Prophetic Affirmations

Bread from Heaven
Prophetic Affirmations

Help Lord, Help!
Prophetic Affirmations

Wake Up and Praise!
An Invitation to Experience God's Glory

Printed in the United States
by Baker & Taylor Publisher Services